Think Big.
Work Hard.
Be Kind.
No Excuses.

by Robert Krumroy

illustrated by Abby Chen

Think Big. Work Hard. Be Kind. No Excuses.

© 2019 Robert Krumroy

All rights reserved. No portion of this book may be reproduced in any form without permission from the publisher, except as permitted by U.S. copyright law. For permissions contact:

Books@KidsDreamsMatterPublishing.com

Cover by Abby Chen and Donna West

ISBN: 978-0-578-46422-0

This is a work of fiction. Names, characters, places and incidents either are products of the author's imagination or are used fictitiously. any resemblance to actual events, locales, or persons, living or dead, is entirely coincidental.

For Zach, today was a typical Monday ... or was it? A new week was starting. The sun was shining. The school bus had just arrived at his stop.

His friends were already on board. Nothing seemed different, but Zach knew something had changed.

Zach thought to himself, "I know I look the same. My clothes are just like any other day. I have my backpack on. I'm sitting in my normal seat, but something inside my head is different." No one could see it, but Zach had made a choice – one that could make his dreams come true.

Zach, thought to himself, "I am going to start thinking BIGGER. I am going to work harder, get better grades, be nicer and never give up. NO more excuses! I know I'm young, but I have BIG dreams and this is the first time I can see them ... in my mind. It's up to me to make it happen!"

Over the weekend, Zach had been with his school friend Alberto at his house. Alberto's older brother, Carlos, a senior in high school was having his 18th birthday party.

Carlos had invited his closest friends. All of them were super nice and all of them were talking about what they were going to do in a few months when they graduated.

One was going to be a policeman, because getting good grades had qualified him to attend the police academy. Another was accepted into a technical school to become an electrician. Four more were going to college to become school teachers, a doctor, a nurse and Carlos was going to be a veterinarian.

They all had big dreams. They had all made good grades and they were all confident about their BIG future. Working hard and getting good grades even when they were younger had made their dreams come true.

They all remembered third grade when the teacher asked everyone what they wanted to be! Everyone in the class was asked to close their eyes and told to try to "see" their dreams in their minds.

To make their dreams come true, they knew they needed to work hard, so every week they encouraged each other to do good. They soon became known as the kindest kids in school ... as well as some of the most successful.

Though they were all older than Zach, Alberto's brother Carlos, asked, "Zach, what do you want to be when you grow up?" Zach wasn't sure. No one had asked him that before.

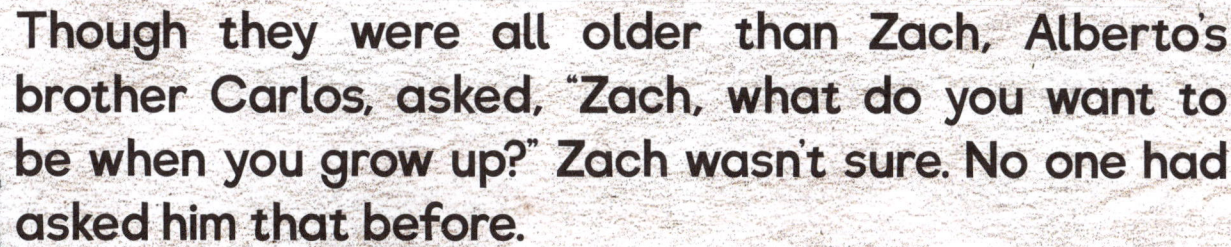

Carlos said, "It's important to think BIG! Don't settle for too little. You can become whatever you want if you start now, work hard, get good grades and never give up, which is exactly what we all did."

Carlos said grades mattered even at my age. He said, "Zach, if you're going to achieve your dreams, getting good grades and working hard starts now, not later.

Our good grades got us into colleges, the police academy and technical schools, which is what you have to do for your dreams to come true."

Alberto said his older brother started making good grades when he was very young. He decided in first grade that he wanted to be a veterinarian so he could care for dogs and cats. He loved animals and knew he would have to go to college to achieve his dream.

That's why he studied, did his homework, got good grades and never made excuses. He was committed to doing good because he knew what he wanted.

What are you going to be when you grow up? A doctor? Nurse? Teacher? Veterinarian? Electrician? If you're really determined to achieve your goal, working hard and getting good grades matter.

Carlos said, "Don't ever make excuses for not working hard or getting good grades. Excuses never matter if you really want your dream to come true. Just decide you're going to do better and do it!"

Zach thought, that's why today is different for me.
I am different!

For the first time, I can SEE my future!
I can become whatever I want if I decide today to think big, work hard, be one of the nicest kids in school and make no excuses.

Why don't you try it, too? Just close your eyes and visualize your dream. Share with others what it is and how you can make it come true.

Questions to Answer

Challenge Questions: 1

1. What does it mean to think BIG?..
....

2. What do you want to be when you grow up?................................
....

3. Why do getting good grades matter?...
....

4. What does it mean to "visualize" your dream?.............................
....

5. What does it mean to work hard? ....
....

6. How do you feel after you have worked hard and been successful?
....

7. Give an example of something you worked hard at and succeeded.
....

8. What should you work harder on in school?................................
....

Challenge Questions: 2

1. How can you be nice to others in school? ....
   ....

2. Give an example of how you can be kind to your parents ....
   ....

3. How can you be kinder to your brothers or sisters? ....
   ....

4. Give an example of how you can be nice to people that you encounter when you're away from home ....
   ....

5. Pick a person in your class that you admire. Write a note about why you admire them and what you think they are really good at doing. (Was this an act of encouragement? How did it make you feel?)
   ....
   ....

Challenge Questions: 3

1. What does it mean to be determined to accomplish something? ....
   ....

2. What does it mean to make no excuses? ....
   ....

3. Who controls what grade you get in class or how well you do a task?
   ....

4. Who determines if you will be successful? ....
   ....

5. What does it mean to encourage others? ....
   ....

6. How can you encourage other students? ....
   ....

7. Give me an example of how you have encouraged someone (written a get-well card, birthday card, complimented them on a good job). How did it make you feel? ....
   ....

Final Assignment: Write a paper

My future dream is to become a/an: ...inventor or a house flipper with my parents...

I chose this because: ....

....

Include how the four items below will help you to achieve your dream:

**Think Big.
Work Hard.
Be Kind.
No Excuses.**